TRAFFIC SAGA

LIA DEWEY MORGAN

AF585256

Other publications by Lia Dewey Morgan

POETRY

Bath Songs

LIA DEWEY MORGAN

TRAFFIC SAGA

CORDITE 06
BOOKS 05

First printed in 2026
by Cordite Publishing Inc.

PO Box 58
Castlemaine 3450
Victoria, Australia
cordite.org.au | corditebooks.org.au

© Copyright Lia Dewey Morgan 2026
© Introduction copyright Lucy Van 2026
Lia Dewey Morgan and Lucy Van assert their rights to be known as the respective author and introducer of this work.

National Library of Australia
Cataloguing-in-Publication:

Morgan, Lia Dewey
Traffic Saga
978-1-7644491-0-6 paperback
I. Title.
A821.3

Poetry set in Lora 10 / 15
Cover design by Zoë Sadokierski
Text design by Kent MacCarter and Zoë Sadokierski
Printed and bound by McPhersons in Maryborough, Victoria

All rights reserved.

This book is copyright. Apart from any fair dealing for the purposes of research, criticism, study, review or otherwise permitted under the *Copyright Act*, no part of this book may be reproduced by any process without permission. Enquiries should be addressed to Cordite Publishing Inc. Cordite Publishing Inc. thanks Alex Creece, Lia Dewey Morgan and Lucy Van for their input during the production of this book.

10 9 8 7 6 5 4 3 2 1

For my dad

CONTENTS

PREFACE

Among trans people, decals on logistics trucks have been a long-standing joke. Taking a selfie beside the TransExpress truck suggests an odd comparison: the queer person as a sort of infrastructure, carrying weight, essentials, the convenience of modern living. The burdens of normality placed upon the marginalised. Ironically then, to be trans often means a restriction of movement. When I finally got a decent job as a trans person, I knew I wanted to travel. I did some soul-searching about my paternal lineage in South Asia, and wanted to learn more about Partition. The contradictions of Indian society threw light on back home Australia; both colonised by the British, India is humiliated by its recent history while much of so-called 'Australia' remains deeply in denial. Here I envisage poetry as a form of reportage, compressing this complexity into something digestible. What unfurls from these years of work-then-travel are wandering verses, across both continents, at bus stops and on planes, filled with the voices of other travellers and migrants, and our collective experiences of being stuck in-between ...

INTRODUCTION

The way the expression 'half your luck' feels luckier than all your luck; the way half-light falls more beautifully than full light; the way halfway around the world sounds further than all the way around. Half: the bisector, but what was the whole? To think like the Indian poet Sujata Bhatt, how far east is still east? Where is the halfway point, what threshold of receptivity yields to our secret question: staying or leaving? Do we find it in 'the informal, unlicensed halfway zone of the parking lot'? Do we find it in the precariously unifying contortions of gods:

> You tell me how Shiva contorted
> the holy crowd's judgement by transcending his form
> uniting with Parvati, becoming half man, half woman
> ('the day of consecration in Ayodhya')

Lunge-stepping magnificently over some abyss, we pause and wonder, why does 'half woman' appear womanlier; earlier, why does 'half-written' sound more authorising than 'written', or 'half-Pakistani' sound more emphatically Pakistani? Is the answer in the curved hand of Morgan's fiat comma, carving up the line: 'We are both the tourist, we are both the guide', or in the 'cigarette apostrophes' that mark the various intermezzos that stage a long coming home? Both. Half your luck.

The way we hum a child into the half-sleep of a long-haul flight. The speaker and the mother share a complicitous nod, for 'I feel it, / start humming too, hmmmmmmmmmmmm / (as long as my breath will allow) hmmmmmmmmmmm'. The jet engine rattles to join them, 'hmmmmmmmm', and the cabin of the plane becomes another meditating membrane between inner and outer words – here is another cavernous mouth vibrating, for engines hum, too, joining mothers, poets, shamans and droning bees in a worldwide hum in that halfway zone between speech and song. Traffic hums its 'saga,' a song that is porous, yes, and chaotic, yes, but never beyond description:

> and I was
> politely muttering
>
> I was still
> within the mouth
> putting words to it
> ('central')

Putting words to it: saga to traffic, sounding a city out, like William Burroughs did when he looked out his window on 7th Street, 'a place where the unknown past and the emergent future meet in a vibrating soundless hum'. Energy and instinct of this in the suburbs, too, where the membranes bounce between the 'shrill call of cicadas' and 'Distracted, listening / to American politics / thinking I don't know'. Knowledge half-knows. Memory passes through smoke. Is it deep? Does it breathe?

The way I don't credential this collection because it beckons another kind of account (though in these brackets I attest the work walks a sharply decolonial edge). It is as if the book were a lung that fills, empties, clears: 'The novelty had gone – and that was desirable.' But what mischief! Novelty abounds! We have been bouncing at what appeared to be normal speed when, in the final section, the title poem drops. Big traffic pushes the dial to 160 bpm: jungle! In the exquisite banality of border crossing! In the half-certainty of itinerary! 'When I say it like that, it sounds both too much and not enough.' Still trafficking, the 'night is collapsing like a vacuum'. The saga 'yanks back to place'. The traffic is ecstatic.

—Lucy Van

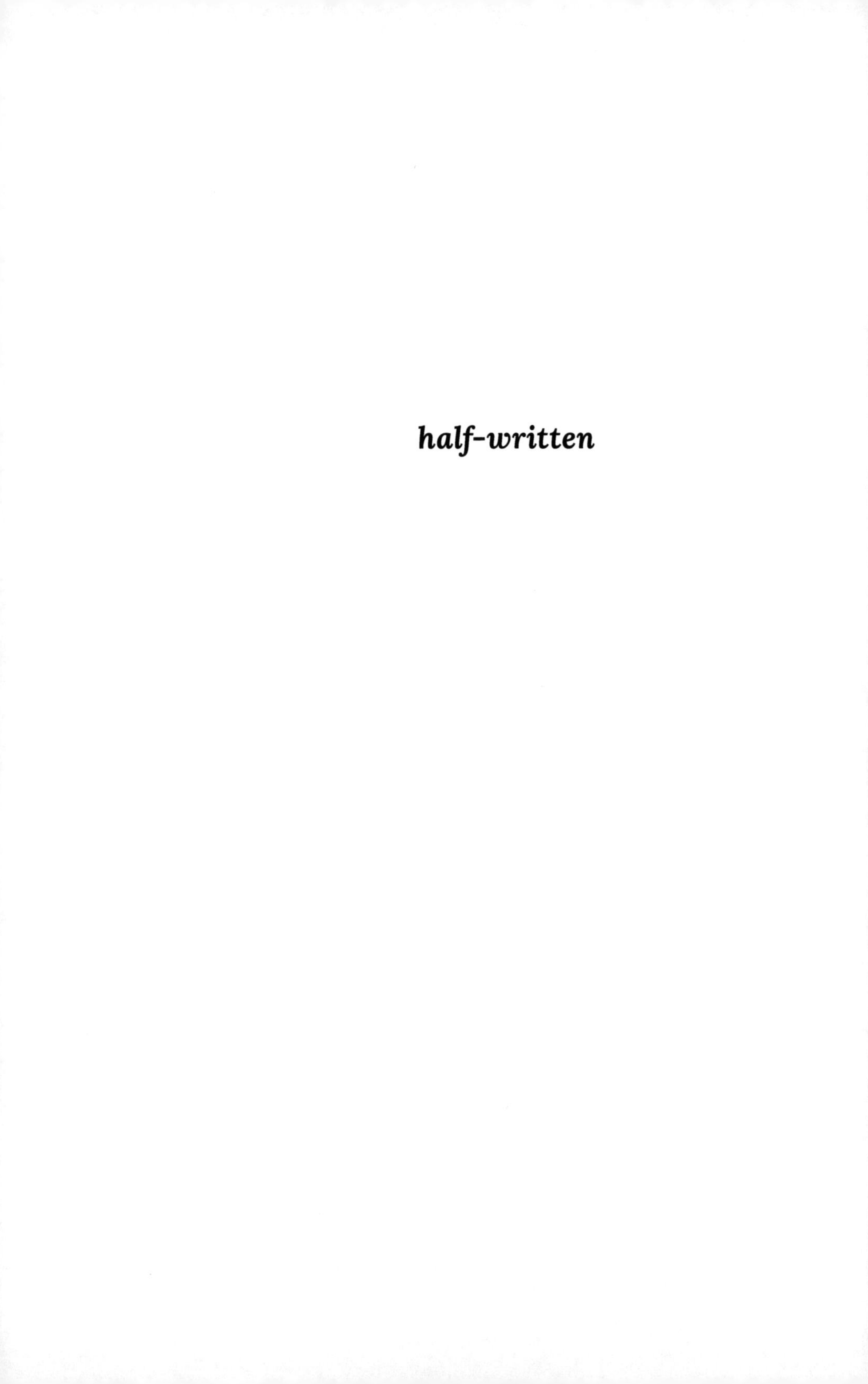

half-written

half-written poem

Here is a poem I cannot write yet:

My father is half-Pakistani.

Sometimes we have to say things
before we know what they mean.

My father is half-Pakistani.

He was adopted by a white family
who liked getting more babies.
They liked brown babies.
They had Jamaicans, Stolen Generation ...

My father is half-Pakistani.
My father insists he has never experienced racism.
My father was in the army band
then the air force band.

My father wanted me to play football.
My father left Mum when I was two
for another woman. He had a suitcase packed
beneath the bed, left in the middle of a fight.

My father is half-Pakistani.
My father will not talk to me about Pakistan.

I like to learn about Pakistan.
I like to learn about all the cultures, all the peoples.
I like to learn about history.

My father insists what has happened
has happened and we must move on.
ACTION STATIONS he used to shout
while rushing me out of the room.

These past few years, we stop speaking.
My father and I are not on speaking terms.

My father is half-Pakistani.
I see him everywhere, dressing like everyone.
He likes to wear puffer jackets with his buzzed bald head
but when he turns around, he is not my father.

I had a dream about my father. He took me
to a pub. We were served too much food:
chicken parmas, steak, chips and a burger.

My father has a beer gut.
My father let me drink Coke.

I remember my father marinating pork ribs
in Coca Cola and cough syrup.
I remember my father taking me to yum cha
trays of colourful jelly, steamed xiao long bao.

My father is half Pakistani.
Mum says he used to cook the spiciest curries.
Mum says he had long hair and loved women.
Mum says he grew dope and flushed it down the toilet.
My grandfather was Pakistani.
He left Pakistan wanting a better life.

He had a fling with a nurse then lost touch.

My father is half-Pakistani.
He was first named David by that white nurse
who called her next child David too.

Sometimes I feel perverse saying any of this – after all
I can't write this poem yet – I told you!

There is a single two-page document that says
everything about where my father and I come from.

It says my great-grandma and grandpa
were Hindu and Muslim, probably North Indian
then the Partition, that great displacement,
pushed them to Pakistan. My great-grandma
died of heartbreak missing her home.

Sometimes I think I feel her heartbreak.
My grandfather left his country.

My father taught me how to make espresso.
My father explained how Melbourne city was planned.

When he left my mother, my father stayed in Hong Kong,
sent me postcards with letters of the alphabet drawn on.

My father loves shooting big cameras at nature.
My father loves finely bred Siamese cats.

My father said my mum feminised me.
I tried to speak to my father like I would my friends.
My father said, 'Your friends must all be women.'
I've forgotten what he said then about being a man.

cicada song

A white cotton bed sheet
hung up on the Hills Hoist
turns with the summer
wind. Christmas approaches.
Visiting my family with you
for the first time, a cicada
has latched on to the sheet
seeming unlikely, special;
my mum strokes its wings
to check if it's still alive ...
At last, it flinches. Normally
I only find the shell left
to inspect in its absence.

A small miracle, a jet
shadowing the yard,
the roar announcing,
Look up and shut up.
For celebrations, we had
cheese, Prosecco and beer
lubricating our gathering.
It was irregular rubbing
the four of us together
at the ends of everything,
our talk echoing round
the rental's high ceiling.
Mostly pleasant, the heat
curled the horizon, but
I still ought to be careful
to spend time alone.

You insisted I take
the afternoon walking
out useless memories
that get in the way. Grass
thick with the forgetting of
December. The path full of
fallen branches, the shrill
call of cicadas growing.
Distracted, listening
to American politics,
thinking I don't know
this country. As a kid,
I went along with the kids
fishing in the storm drain
here. All this city's rivers
cemented like mum's yard.

We fished out a shoe – cliché.
I forgot all their names.
I follow the trickle past
topless boys shooting hoops,
along the old aqueduct
always useless in my lifetime
to the Wangal country mural
mob fishing beneath a jet
silhouette cast in galaxies.
Cars dream past the flaky
paint shadowed by scaffolding –
perhaps it is on its way out
and won't be there next visit.

Mostly alone, every few months
I come to see my family,
end up walking quite a lot
to clear my confused head.
I keep up with the prosecution
of the president: these old crimes
sure aren't mine but make me feel
things are normal. I don't understand
the proceedings, crossing worn roads
Mum drove me down to school.
Now the new concrete structures
jut planter green, so much grey.

I used to come here swinging
round the harbour to reach old
horse sheds where I jigged class.
After a long dream eating fish,
I snuck out with my first love
          and ate her cunt right here
                    among the fig roots.
Gone,   dilapidated glory.
          A developer replaced it
with gourmet dining. I do
not like visiting, but once
I did go in to buy a beer –
I didn't know where I was!
Now I just keep walking ...

Housesitting: the cat runs off
after his meal. Everything stinks
of sandstone thick with moss.

I catch a bus home down luscious
hills where old crushes lived.
          Is ageing always like this?
I talk to you about it all, and
you've never moved cities, now
you're fantasising about moving
here, flicking through our phones
in my parents' queen-sized bed.

I board the aeroplane with you.
The flight was delayed because
of shit weather. About to land
from my first to my second home
and neither home is really home.
Rubbing the thoughts together
between my empty hands, buzzing
engine, the controlled shriek of
landing wheels extending into
grey. Acceleration. Acceleration.

central

There was **IMMORTAL**
painted across the hallways
of Central's mouth

Rows of little teeth
took intrepid bites
of foreign foods

Crepes, roe, salmon
larger than life slabs
of chocolate hung over

The portrait of a demon
extruding as passers-by
rushed to opportunities
of exquisite becoming

Model families
self-iterated, well-bred
puppies domesticated
into restrained behaviours

Going home to play
murder games, enacting
precise decisions
enabled by advertisements

and I was
politely muttering

I was still
within the mouth
putting words to it

I was sat
eating the item
described on the menu

I was licking
my lips for a moment
they all entered me

The periphery reflected
the organising principle

A preacher
proclaimed The One Book
facing a library

Deciduous leaves
co-mingled with rubbish

Beneath real estate listings
the homeless slept

A great deal of faces
to not remember

Disposable bags
with large brand names
crossed when the lights
flashed verdant

And strange
chaotic interactions
beyond description

Teens flee shopping
centre transport hub
bashing the security tag
of the brand new Nikes

and I was
waiting for you

I was watching
not interfering
or interacting

I was seen
by you, I had to
take a few steps

towards myself
out from them
away from here

drum

ENJOY THE WILDERNESS
        says the bus stop
        white lotto ad woman
gripping her cup of hot fiat

Black men under shelter
drink   avoid rain

I have   a drum of olive oil
for a set. Missing tooth man
looks me up n down, asks
            how's your day?

Wearing camouflage
jacket n track pants
I must look like a man
I must look approachable

So we talk, his friend
        asks in language
(he translates)   *what's your name?*
                  A girl's name

So I tell him   I'm transgender
he says *white people got too much*
freedom   *have to look for trouble*

Bus comes, I lift up
dinner for a fortnight
Say   Well   Wishes
Go   Home   Alone

the english half

'Are you from   ?'

'   '

'I was there in 2018!'

'   '

'Beautiful country – so sad what has happened.'

'   '

'So, where in   are you from? MAIN CITY?'

'   '

'Well, you're here now.'

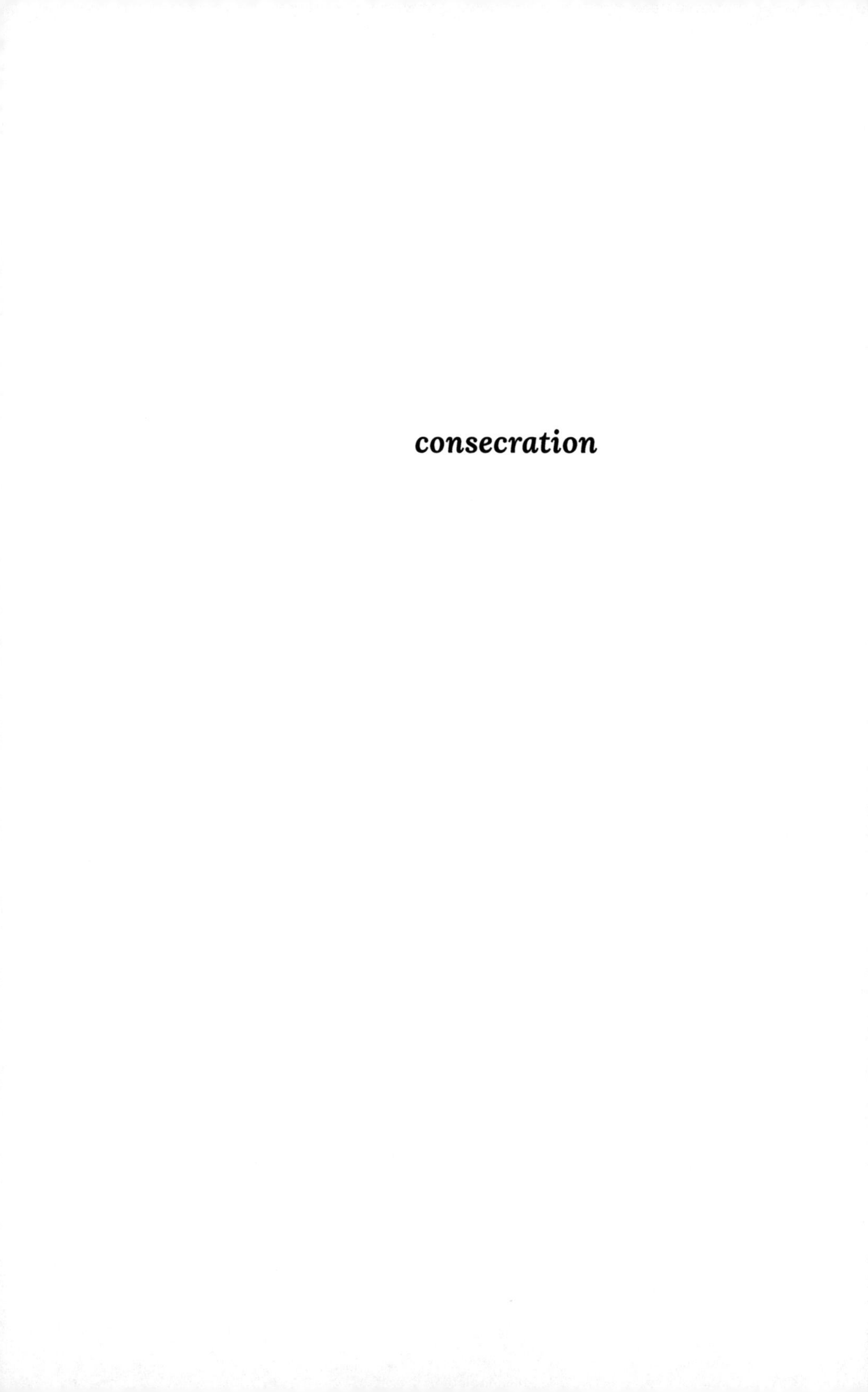

consecration

blue stone onam

And so it was, Sunday afternoon
stoned walking aimless, blue sky
and yellow sun falling over
a Presbyterian church I'd never
seen before. A couple with a pram
dressed King of Trainers, conservative
like bald men shouting Hail Maries
down King Street. Like influencer selfies,
or the woman next to you at the cafe
who shrieks suddenly, laughing.
I averted my eyes, not wanting to
stare or cause them discomfort.

It was a funny time to be trans
with a Christian. My new friend and I
got coffee at the old Greek cafe
where cakes sit behind shiny glass.
She took a photo of her cappuccino
then asked what I was doing this
weekend. 'Maintenance.' She would
visit a new church, the one next to
the station. I could remember faces
of thc buildings, but never entered.
Told her, 'My mum was raised devout
but broke away, raised me without

religion,' passing the Old Magistrates'.
I thought about what to tell her; what
could be shared in the space between
us; what might shock her or just
go over her head, be misunderstood.

After all, it wasn't her first language –
it was maybe her third or fourth.
She had designed buildings for Saudis,
finished college in Kerala. I suppose
this was ordinary to someone else
but to me it was still so new. I asked
simple questions, 'What's that like?'

I had spent my life struggling with friends
who found communicating confusing
sometimes. I noticed people connecting
with me were torn between different
identities. Another colleague and friend
had grown up between East and West,
just now understanding how strongly
it impacted her as a child. The stories
run together in my mind, as we walked
alongside the Old Melbourne Gaol. Heavy
stone bricks and groups of tourists, back

into the clammer of festivities: golden saris,
rainbow rice pookalam, tessellating prayers
of rolling Desi girls. A dancer balanced on
a copper plate, her ankle bells ringing out as
she shuffled here and there. Another dancer
leaned over to explain to me the pageantries:
how a generous king made a god so jealous,
he stomped the king down into a nether realm.
Now he returns once a year, bringing peace,
bringing harvest. I told her, 'I'm grateful to
take part in such culture and tradition – we
don't have much of that here.' I imagined

visiting a queer club together. It'd be late
for starters – that alone could put her off.
The techno would sweat loudly. I doubt
she'd tried drugs before. Like a heathen
I felt, like bad propaganda about Western
homosexuals corrupting our children. But
that was the muck where I found myself first
I wanted to share with love. Suppressed,
uncertain how to open up appropriately
when the fruits of this life were strange,
taboo. Still, it was my nature to be polite,
taking pride in how I comfort strangers.

Her shoulders afloat in a strapless sundress
and I in a borrowed kurta, block-printed
with leaves of turquoise, green and pink
blossoms. We glowed like flowers. I was
a little nervous, assuming others stared
but here you were being kind, being gentle.
I wondered if that was your Christian side
or if that was a little reductive. We cheered
together as lines of men and women swung
in choreographed ecstasy synchronised to
Malayalam pop hits, crowd singing along.
The sky was blue, the sun quite warm.

Le Corbusier did not plan New Delhi

I have been here before, the real
official office *not fake?* he asks
the man in English, then bickers on
in Hindi   huge map spread across
the desk: pictures of white people
on camels, tigers, the Taj Mahal
Tea? I say no, he asks again, nono
(he'd just told me not to accept tea
from strangers in Delhi – one tourist
woke up, lost all his possessions ...)
I say no again. He asks   *where*
do you come from? fuck, I have to
say it again – australia***Cricket!!***
where do I come from?   *where*
    do you want to go? the Punjab
        trying to pronounce it properly
he answers, *what you want to do there?*
            I'll go to the Partition museum
        his eyes sharpen, he keeps talking
        the Golden Temple, two days
then you go down to Rajasthan
go to Goa, Varanasi   I need to go
I say sorry I'm sorry to waste your time
these men always sweet sweet chai until
furious   he yells, *don't be sorry this*
is business!   I go downstairs, thick with
pollution, light a cigarette, offer my new
friend one. He smokes,   *sorry bro I know*
they were trying to rip you off, I'll tell you
                it's because you look like tourist
you need to buy Indian clothes, you'll look
            like second Indian, let me show you

a place – not like these other places
where you take the cloth from out
the underground knot of no fixed price
wash it once, it falls apart – no, I know
a real good place, come with me
chalo! around the corner,
the door shuts, mutes horns, a man
sitting behind a long glass cabinet
beneath a wall of plastic-wrapped
kurtas: peach, aqua, patterned
what is your favourite colour
let me show you one more thing
this one is reversible, you see blue
on one side, black on the other
specially designed, Kashmiri
pashmina, hand-stitched, fine quality
7,200 *rupee* – I do a quick division
in my head. That is too much, blush
apologise. He insistently shows me
another, another, *just tell me a price*
I will not be offended. I offer him
less than half (haggler's law), has to
ask the boss, stern in a linen thobe
he approves, but insisting, walks me
over to the jewellery, *when you mine*
you don't know what you'll discover
topaz, ruby, emerald – I want

to leave, I count crumpled
notes, get out before he sells
me more, I'm told he's frustrated
I know how to bargain, the clothes
fall apart as soon as I get home

saint-soldier (sant-sipahi)

I was once again litigating the case of
Palestinian resistance to a Jewish mother
who felt there was a double standard,
sending me pictures of her relatives
once exiled from Yemen, asking me, *please*
do not share these with others. It tears me
up to disagree with friends who I love
so I bicker in my head back and forth trying
to hold her truth, hold mine, hold it all together

as the guard in royal purple looked down
on me sternly. I tucked away my phone
looking out again towards the nectar
of the Golden Temple: pilgrims compacted
together in long beams of spectral cloth
guided by criss-crossing bannisters. Devotees
waited several hours – I was new to all this,
still mimicking gestures of how to pray:
touch the floor then my forehead. A headless
man carries his own head and shining sword
as pilgrims collapse before him in quiet prayer.

I had a cheap blue brochure, **Breakfast with**
God, that said the burden was endless, so
awake, fight the good fight, fight and win!
I folded it back in my kurta pocket, circling
through women in a spectrum of phulkari
suits and Sikh men naked dipping their
bodies deep in holy water. I knew nothing
of the Panjabi verses shaking the complex
with tablas and sarangi clawing at god.

I only knew how to say thanks in bad Hindi,
how to bow my head low, pressing my hands
together in prayer towards them, towards them,
and another, another again – everything so
beautiful, it was easy to focus. Eventually
after walking barefoot across the polished
marble, I turned to the gurdwara's langar,
joining a long queue before the thundering
clammer of pots and pans. Rattling steel
plates were handed out, along with spoons
and bowls for water. On long hessian aisles

crossed legs, lentils, potato, rice, pudding
was spooned out from above. To receive
we held out our open hands, hot bread
slapped upon our skin. The water trolley
stopped and started before each pilgrim
as men walked the aisles   calling *dahl*
dahl   *chawal chawal*   *pani pani* forever
offering more. Slowly, we departed for
a long queue of dirty dishes, donations,
dipped our toes in renewed ablutions, went
back to our circling prayers. Thoughts

still swirling in me about victimhood,
about being religious. A long museum
of Sikh sacrifices, wars and martyrs sat
in the wing of the temple, each with a name
and fate: Shaheed Bhai Jai Singh who was
skinned to death by Mughals for refusing
to carry a bag containing a king's smokes.

What is the cost of continuing culture?
It could be an issue with the translation,
but plates commemorated big Holocausts
I'd never heard of: '84, when the temple burnt,

yet another justification to carry a knife
tucked in the turban, one more by the ankle.
A syncretic religion that discovered opponents
surrounding them. Lines were drawn through
the people, leaving the faithful to peer
at pilgrimage sites through binoculars.
I left the temple backwards, touching
for one last time, the floor, my forehead,
the two sides of my temple, and went back
to the hostel's rooftop, littered with smokes.
Swiping Instagram stories of *not in my name.*
I had no religion, an atheist again, watching
children fly kites in the polluted sky. They asked
what country you from?   *how long you here?*

the day of consecration in Ayodhya

1

Today is the day of consecration in Ayodhya
that potent symbol of a new Indian warrior
nationalism that divides crowds into roaring
Rams and weeping Sufis bedraggled in rags

Some months earlier: every day at work, I took
to reading Indian news, which began obscure
in a shroud of Delhi smog, but slowly the noise
subsided; in a dilapidated courtyard, we calmly

learnt about Dalits, Muslims, eunuchs. A pitter
patter of violence in my newsfeed, even after
waves of censorship. I visited in dry season, still
it was raining and we waited in the cool bar.

The rain cleared. A local offered me the back
of his motorbike. We went to the next town,
the next, each with multiple glaring Modis
and at the train station, Modi selfie stations.

On life went, I think – the walls of Delhi had been
torn down and reconstructed many times over.
Everyone from traders to invaders had become
Indian at last. Christ was Krishna, Persia Parsi

bells rung beside calls to prayer, all burning
the same incense, all tying string from a single
spool. Men gathered in the night to sing ghazal,
each taking their turn: Hindi songs, Urdu songs,

women in modesty wear clapping along, hands
twirling from front to back, keeping the time.
Eventually, even us foreigners were called up
to sing whatever song we might remember ...

In a yellow room thick with beards and sweet
smoke, I was told the lesser-known history of
how the fabric of Calicut was cut, a time before
the Europeans. Land was parcelled out between

every trader who came by monsoon. Yemeni
mosques, Assyrian Orthodox churches, Chinese
and every other spice, dye, grain, root rested
on the heads of Big Bazaar Road. Ornate trucks

in the blistering speed of a palm-tree shoreline,
a Dutch house was converted by an offshore
project member of Google Street View, to serve
all black specialty coffee grown in the hills.

Here I finished reading Attar's *Memorial of the Saints*:
a Sufi despairs when he tumbles downstairs,
if only there'd been a few more steps, for every
injury was a kiss pressed upon him by God.

I closed the old world in a book as I grew high on
caffeine, sneaking cigarettes in the dark passage
beside the cafe. There was no public smoking
in Kerala, just staring uncles and abrupt judgement.

2

I see you enter, sunny scarf, chequered blue and
orange button-up searching the cafe's bookshelves,
flipping through Márquez and Rumi. I'm saying to you,
ohhh, so you're into mystical poetry, magical realism.

You're saying to me, *ohhh, so you're spiritual.* We sit
on the floor together. You tell me how Shiva contorted
the holy crowd's judgement by transcending his form,
uniting with Parvati, becoming half man, half woman.

It's twenty minutes – not even half an hour – before
you must leave. We just *have* to get coffee. Leaving me
with your contacts, I am shocked. I immediately write
a poem about you. Your first message is love hearts.

Our first date the next day there are butterflies
in the garden by the museum, couples on swings.
We start holding hands while trying to cross the road,
linking pinkies and then, maybe, something more.

Walking through Pazhassi Raja, cannonballs get bigger
as the years pass by. The tombs become more elaborate.
I notice you like to take photos of me, among the old
pieces of ceramic vessels. Then, you take me out to dinner

at the newly opened floor of Paragon. I'm not so graceful
eating biryani and fried fish with my hands, but I guess
you find it endearing. I watch with delight at how precise
your fingers press raita, papad and rice. Beside each other
we wash our hands. You teach me to wash my mouth

after meals. *We drink tap water back home*, I say
and you're grossed out. I tell you so many little things,
you tell me you want to hear it all. You tell me about how

you never wanted to travel overseas, really. Everyone else
wants to leave for Canada or Dubai, but you're more of
an Indian sanskari girl. Despite this, you tell me you'd like
to see where I live, just because I come from there,

because it's a part of me. You post a photo of me
with the words, *my soul met yours today*, telling me,
I think ... we are soulmates. I think so too. It is crazy
I am in India smoking Indie Mints (you smoke them)

on my balcony thinking of you. Another midnight here,
I saw a large unidentified rodent in the foyer while
I was covered in ants. Now I am in love. You gifted
to me a trishula pendant, that symbol of the Destroyer.

I bought a chain for it to hang on my neck. Rubbing
the trident when I miss you, I call my mother
to check if I have lost my mind. I have not. I want
to turn my world upside down for you. As the sun sets

again and again over Calicut beach, we eat local food
you've never tried before: pazhampuri and beef.
I walk you down laneways you haven't seen.
We are both the tourist, we are both the guide,

we are equals. We are both stared at by the uncles
as we try to find somewhere to smoke in peace, walking
through a group of children looking for privacy, then
we are chased by angry dogs for stepping on

their territory. Young boys start heckling me for
500 rupees. Something is being said in Malayalam
that you don't know how to translate, making you feel
distressed. We hide at the back of the cafe holding

hands, a stumbling conversation giggling at language
breaking down. You are worried how others will see us,
how they judge me as a tourist and will tell your family
about our love. We decide on the code word *language*,

which you say when you need me to pretend, to live
in this empire of secrets. We link pinkie fingers, barely
connected, and yet ... Oh, and yet! We make so many
promises together! We are two mad women in love!

Today is the day of consecration in Ayodhya. On Instagram,
a co-worker of mine posts a video shouting, *Jai Shree Ram!*
while another posts a celestial graphic of Ram captioned,
If you've never had your country taken away from you

you wouldn't understand this day. Both are vegetarians
living outside India, insisting that I am wrong to share a post
on how the nation is celebrating the destruction of a mosque.
We meet up and are both a little tense, upset that I am leaving,
so we sit on the hotel rooftop, smoking again, a little joint

with some Indian reggae. The adhan calls, a tricolour flag
bigger than our bodies pressed together waves in the sunset.
You whisper, *my India is something else* ... The moon sinks
into the sky, an adrift parasol, a cut kite, Shiva's toenail ...

coming home

took several days
took seventy hours
of being alone with weight and time

The cigarette apostrophes
luggage left aside and eating
to kill time

Coming home took several months
a lifetime ago

Coming home took a lifetime of being
alone with weight and time

The dizzy trip across time zones
climates she is asleep on the couch when
I get home

There were two train stations
three auto rickshaws a spiralling coffeehouse
three airports Ilaiyaraaja in a juice-shack
the picture of the dargah in my backpack,
the Qur'an the Adi Granth the Therigatha
and many jangly little jhumka and perfumes
destined to others' hands

I was delirious and calling you
all the time, pretending
that our pinky fingers
were still interlinked

Facing out the open door
of a moving train
facing a swamp
the sweaty in and out of sleep

It had already been tragic
it was time to walk and find
somewhere discreet to smoke
HEY *this is Private Property!*

Why are you smoking here?
Walk with so much weight somewhere else
the day involved a series of operations
coming home took a series of operations

At each exit I cry baby:
The final day   The night before   The morning of
Leaving the station   Arriving at the airport
On the first plane   At the airport   On the second plane

While getting off the bus
Finally walking back home
I cry   I cry   I cry   I cry

        I had looked at you with the sincerest desire
        to have everything understood overturned
        I sought destruction, you offered a trishula

I wanted you under my skin
months later as I write this
you call me   witchcraft
telepathy, being soulmates,
two Leos born a day apart
were all on the cards

                                        fuck, you were beautiful

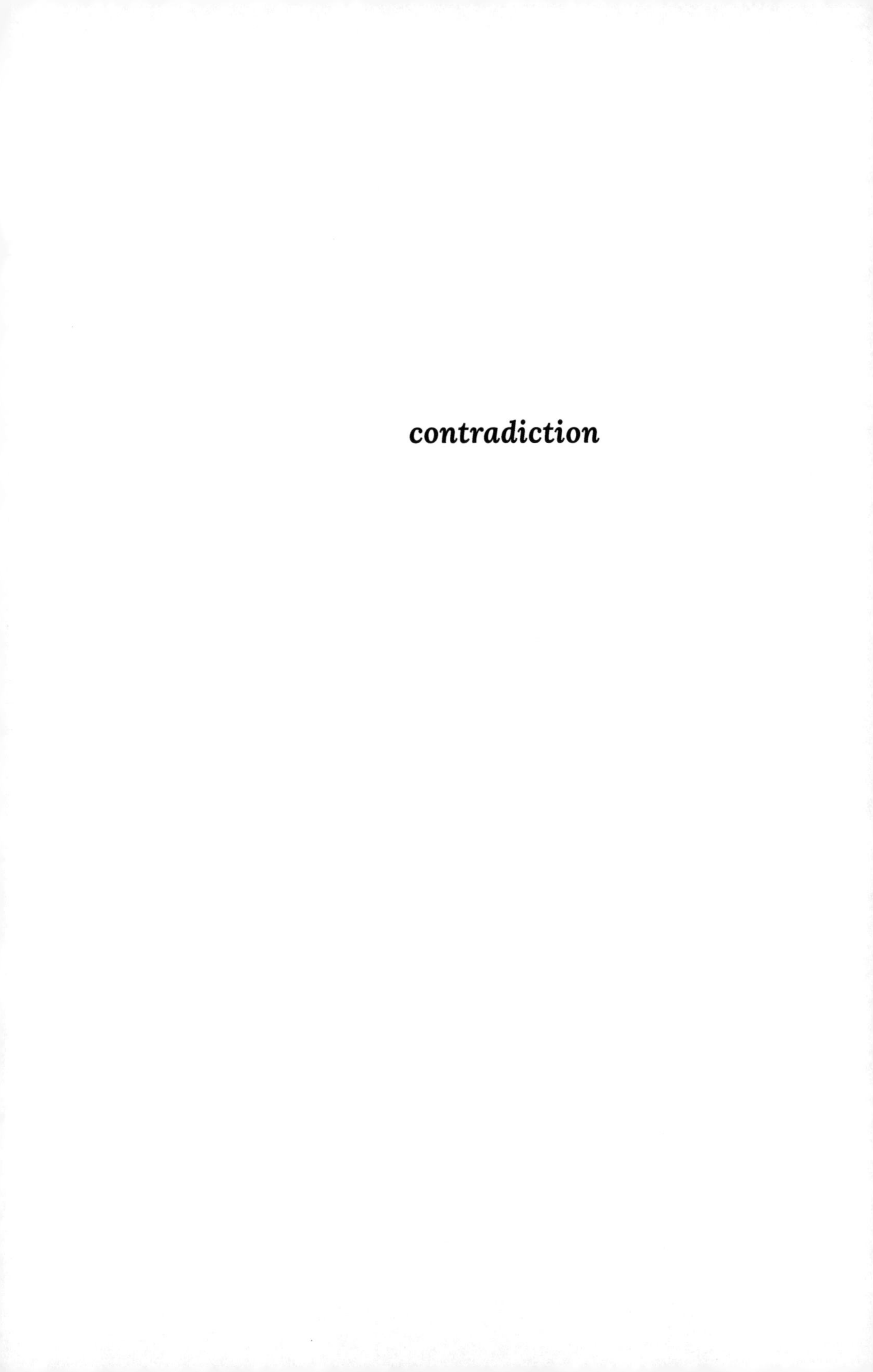

contradiction

ghosts

come out on the peak hour bus
        the   MY DAD *was* QUARTER *Aboriginal*
                in army fatigues   dawn drunk
        rattling   *Indigenous folk'll*
protect us in the next war   *Samoans, Papuans*
                        Māori   *they know how to use guns!*
n scuse me, I don't mean to be racist but
                white people don't know how to fight

        descendent of Fuzzy Angels on the bus
with that always soft smile offers me a seat (
comes out abruptly   his family in the jungle
all killed)   *That war is endless but at least*
        its respectable   *no killing womenchildren*
it's about land – IT'S ALWAYS *about* WOMEN!

the other shouts past   the uncomfortable
                tensed white woman cat tattoo'd blue t-shirt
                a pixel art GameBoy **CLASSICALLY TRAINED.**
The *blonde* blonde with *p e r f e c t* foundation
headphones in scrolling TikTok filing her nails

Tommy says   *time is speeding up*
        I remember '93   *I was in grade 1*
        but these clocks are not what you think
        They don't just count time   *they steal it!*
    I could be 36   39   42   it's a quarter to eight
I'm late   whatever,   I'll get to work

            until it is time   to leave again
            they BETTER GIVE YOU *that fucking* VISA

Tommy *I'll steal a yacht*
Tommy, *I'll fly to Cairns steal you a super yacht*
bring you back here *get you that visa Tommy*
we'll sell the YACHT *for a few hundred* THOUSAND

Tommy getting apologetic, tryna keep him quiet
fuck Nick *we missed our stop*
all I could hear was you fuckn talkn I couldn't
focus and I tell'em pointing past
cement a mega church graffiti the market
is back there your next best stop
is just up here catch the train back

like we're mates he asks for my number he's new
to town I lie my phone is dead and I ain't
got a pen sorry the lie passes quick
ALL *I wanted was* CHICKEN WINGS
and they're off the bus I'm off to work

the contradictions were incessant

I rarely leave my bedroom door open
        but this morning I woke to my cat
                chewing on a plastic bag beneath me

When I woke up, an hour before work
        you had messaged, *no secrets xxx*
                that's a pretty good present, and there

it sat beside a message from a Gazan
        or someone exploiting them, 'please share' ...
                fuck these days could be heartbreaking.

Half-joking, a friend or acquaintance's
        story: *now is not the time for brunches*
                now is the time to regret you are born

and yearn ... the coldest winter in years,
        two mega Cs, a Vitamin D gel cap,
                chop chop to smoke and messaging

had got me through the worst of it.
        My mum cried when she found out
                the house had no heating, was worried

to hear about the local factory fire.
        At the opening, we hold hands looking at
                the gigantic painting of Bella Hadid

and her lover fucking. The artist stands
        on a bench charging their glass of wine
                performing a poem. On either side of them

two strangers – women – yell abruptly
        insulting one another across the crowd.
                Afterwards, we all agree it was iconic,

the chartreuse and turquoise glasswork
        perfectly matching the aggressive fucking.
                I noticed a pattern of me visiting the ER,

says another, crashing from a mania, someone I
        used to fuck ... You show me photos of before
                and your eyes are different, your dress wild.

Man buying wine has the sharpest jean pockets
        I've ever seen. We leave, and each crossing
                is an excuse for kisses. I like how we both

get clammy hands. We walk the nighttime
        business quarters, you deliberating where
                you'd be happy to install a big bronze.

Some rain starts coming down, you tell me
you can't have a scarf moment – really
that'd be cultural appropriation. I encourage

you, steal from the French. I found out just
the other day, Flinders Street was designed
to be built in India. I have seen shit on the floor

here, right next to these steel ribbons fencing
scratched-up sandstone – pushing me back,
I grab your hip. We kiss. We kiss. We kiss.

I take you up to the gates, and when you leave
as I roll a cigarette, a man with half a dozen
speakers, helmets, half his house strapped

to his body plays Future. I start acting mean
like I do when I'm alone, in the city, a trans
woman with a bow on her head ...

false alarm

Since I started working here
I've been waiting for the siren

Sometimes, the computer's
start-up noise or a forklift
reversing sounds similar

and I stand, being the face
for anyone to encounter

being the help, being the hand
of a large-scale operation

> Can I help you?
> *Where's the bathroom?*
>
> *I'm looking for a quiet*
> *place to study ...*
>
> *Help me please. How*
> *to get a printout?*
>
> *Where do I find a fountain*
> *to fill up my water bottle?*
>
> *Do you have this book on*
> *mathematics for engineers?*

and chat with colleagues
who fall asleep in the office

dreaming about their weekends
deep in the forest playing guitar

It is 2pm, it is time
for my second coffee,

check Teams, check Outlook,
check the news, check the time

fix a print jam, turn on a monitor,
go to the staff room. Stop to help

a student. Redirect them
to the appropriate service

How do I print here?

Can you help me print?

Where does the print go?

The printer isn't working!

Excuse me, I'm having trouble pri– ***WOOP***
WOOP *remain*
WOOP *where*
WOOP *you*
WOOP *are*

stop what I am doing
don a fire warden vest

rays of the sun god

There I am   dad smiling   his wife
shaved her head   dating a bull
dyke. He's into it   I say hello
to my lost brother   little awkward
but it's warm   homely   finally
behind them a matriarch with dad's skin
burnt sugar regal, beaming, proud — wake

up   alarm calling me to work.
I couldn't decide what to wear,
it grew confusing how to dress
a moustache   a skirt to my ankles
dangling a handbag from my elbow
rushing with the sun to catch the bus
in between workers   get my book.

To be alone reading   allowed to think
was how I found myself   in doubt
misunderstanding terms   not knowing
why I was learning something. This was
home: enough boredom to focus before
the world throws me back into process
work   take questions   give directions.

Between the patrons   I sneak pages
of Ramakrishna's pluralistic theology;
the alterity of South Asian Sufi shrines.
I stop   push chairs, reset a password

connect them   to wi-fi, help them print,
where to get help   with their studies.
I am always smiling try speaking simply

I walk with them   when they are lost.
Regulars smile and nod   as they pass,
bright *Hello again!*   There are patrons
so stressed, I guide them through panic

attacks. Weekends, I wake to ferocious
meowing   coffee   a quiet raga
a chapter or two   ginger cat pushing
into my lap.   Little moments
barely leave the mouth. Contradictions,
coincidences   simultaneities ...
Old friends lost touch, moved house.
Each summer was hotter, winter severe.

It was all breaking. I had to understand
the petrification of knowledge, putrid rays
of the sun god. Sexless for most of the year
I barely knew who to talk to, what to say ...
eating god's word   made rice and stew
for the Beloved, submitting to strange days
where nature   is cut   in many halves.

A broken phallus   buried   watered
transformed   made anew.   Even
matter is metaphor   bodies strewn across
the screen,   reminded I could be a word
even less,   barely a dot of ink in a   0.
Glum humdrum days lent themselves to
bashing one's head against a wall of truth,

just like that,   a work week repeats.
On my knees in stacks quickly scanning

rows of architectural theory. The minutiae
of Trump's legal case on one headphone,
jargon washing   an erroneous baptism.
There's a sort of pleasure in this density
of information, falling into another's life work,

converge   multitask   omnipresent paths.
Elderly physics   staff member renews
a book of equations   he had for five years
a young doctoral candidate   wants sources
on PTSD in the diaspora Japanese textbooks
a Dutch document delivery   Chinese artists
use of red   novels to improve one's English.

I need quiet   where is the bathroom   do you
have a pen?   Of course! Just bring it back
prying bent staples   out of the stapler
a stand-in for poor signage: guiding them
down the hallway   continuous yawning
improvement abyss   stapler breaks again
a blockchain innovation hub   AI rollout
strategy,   students still get pissed off when

pages don't stay together   log out, pack up
call Mum. *How's it going, darling*? Fridays
not so much about what is said   we call.
I'm far away   she's close to home
she misses me. What are you doing for dinner,
Mum? *Salmon kedgeree*. I'll pick up biryani
on my way home, both eating golden rice ... Oh!
Before I go, let me tell you about this dream –

revision

past tense

I stopped shaving my upper lip today.
In two weeks, it'll be *some* moustache
in the steady Georgetown heat, wet with
storms every day – that's the forecast!
Amazing how stable the weather seems
everywhere else, but here, we forgot the
seasons. As a young man, I longed to for-
get myself, under a train or in vipassana.
When I finally got a hold of myself, I'd shed
so much, I was a woman. Sublimation ...

It was eight years ago Trump got voted in
and we had tickets to Kathmandu. I'd
never seen men with so much luggage,
coming from the Gulf states, so wide
eyed, standing and gasping as the plane
passed peaks of Himalayas. We go on
a hike, meet two Silicon Valley media
professionals, passing kid goats, tea
houses where they make lasagne with
curry powder and yak cheese. We chat
about what America feels like. Nostalgic ...

My parents honeymooned here, after Mum
fell off a balcony right before marriage.
She wrote letters that took months to
arrive, now I'm here texting her pictures:
the snowfall on a nameless peak. When
we break up, I get the *Life of Buddha*
thangka, you keep mandalas and plants.
We had travelled every year, four years
in a row; this is what we did together:

watched Al Jazeera in the winter, then
avoided Christmas in sticky Asia. Odd ...

I still remember the crack on the ceiling
of the hotel where you told me, the last
time you *really* meant it, 'I could never
leave you, I love you so much.' We broke
up as soon as I shaved my beard. I didn't
travel for years after that – that beard
that Muslim men loved to come up and
stroke, *Mashallah! You should convert!*
I loved it; sometime later, I loved going
to Daydreams, where everyone sniffed
poppers and pretended it was Berlin. I
would wear bright, silly dresses – youth!

The last time I really remember soaking
a dress, in sweaty exertions, pink with
sequins, was when DJ N**** Fox played
Angolan drums to a closed club, everyone
focused, the stage all ripe with women
outnumbering the DJ ten to one. Fuck. I must
admit most of my best sexual experiences
were by myself. After transitioning, I became
especially good at phone sex, making wet
one slyly masculine woman after another,
year after year. They objectified me! I'd say
to all of them, *I'd die to swap our genitals
as we please.* After a while, I started to see
the power dynamics of the relationships
I was in: hidden, rarely described. Gayyy ...

After my initial enthusiasm for queer
theory I stopped my reading – although
they were trans, it didn't mean I related,
and anyway, not all cis women go about
studying up on feminism. To be free meant
my transness didn't define me. I always
preferred learning about other cultures,
governments, genocides, liberations …
I gave up on my boobs growing to the size
I wanted them, or wearing certain outfits
I'd dreamt of for years. My femininity was
real, despite those who called me 'him'
to the utmost confusion of my girlfriends.

When you have broad shoulders and want
to look like a woman, it's good to play into
your masculinity a little – like a polo dress,
or a nice white blouse. Looking the problem
in the face. Six months of working customer
service, I started feeling obliged to dress
more feminine than I do on my days off.
My vocal register is significantly higher
when I am at work. I don't do it consciously.
Some say my gender is obvious, for others
it is obviously not. Few of us know how
we are seen by others, but some of us must
know more than most. Last time in India

there was one moment I faintly remember
on a train: a teenager, rough, sneaking
cigarettes through the open door turned

towards me asking,   *Are you man*
or woman …   *Man or woman?* No one
really just approached me out of the blue
like that – in English at least – the whole trip.
I'm still confused why it didn't happen more,
but honestly, even with a handful of breast
tissue, a moustache was enough. Normality …
The pencil moustaches of gender bent
AFABs told me it was time to get really
comfy with my womanhood – it was time
to be masculine! I'll get on a plane, forget
where I'm from, and surrounded by men,
travel alone in white shirt, slacks, a secret
stash of hormones in my pack as I hail
an auto rickshaw. He'll look me up-down
thinking, *Ah yes! I have the perfect story*
for this man – I'll tell him the time I fucked
a Russian woman! I'll nod, I won't laugh,
but I'll tell you all about it later. The world
keeps going … I'm writing in past tense.

today you will lose yourself at the beach for Ella

The kids here come each night to find
themselves again, chit-chatting with the
waves, motorbikes pulling in and out,
drifting through hard-worn lanes made
for an ancestor who did a job now gone.

We build artificial lakes, float carved-out
swans with carefully packed lunches and
call this romance. Lake View. Sea Queen.
After work repeats a thousand times, we
save up wishes to go cruising international.

What is a boat but a bridge? And it ain't
always pretty either – the Sydney Harbour
Bridge fucked off a lot of slums just to get
shit-hot famous. Cool ... I like to imagine
businessmen slitting throats with oyster

shells coveted like gemstones, pretty things
sparkling nude in the champagne salted
sea. When you wanna up the price, say
'sea-salt', 'ocean-front property'. In trading
towns we exchange goods, names, licking

lips and fingers after the richness of a meal.
The Malabari sadya lays a hundred curries
out on a banana leaf – traders came here,
named their ship after the coast, wrecked it
into the sandstone between Maroubra and

Long Bay. I'm sure the lasers have pointed
out from the Malabar in India to Malabar,
Sydney seeking connection. Last night, one
DJ kept flipping techno into a psytrance
bass as drunk Muslim youths screamed

in ecstasy. Wedding Cake Island. The Gap.
Let the waves dump you baby, your limbs
discombobulated, accidentally swallowing
cuttlefish piss – yeahhh that's your fucking
ancestors baby! We never left the sea ...

world record largest bust!

If everything is sacred
then even a sham guru
can lead to salvation
by way of the sewer.
Oh, what a beautiful
world we shit in. A high
class mall where the
bidet doesn't reach
my ass, I wash myself
left hand. A whole wall
of shelves dustful and
empty in the bookstore.
Only the really big
publishers stocked there ...
Now in damp colonial walls
the philosophy shelf brims
with Vedas, scriptures,
Bibles, and Ambedkar
is jammed next to Modi's
autobiography. My dorm
mate thinks India would
be better under autocracy,
falls in love with Chinese
roads. I still found my trip
today worthwhile even if
I'm suspicious of meditation
theme parks! How glorious
that God can still be built
in 2017. I order a towel
and yoghurt at 9pm for
₹400. *Money is lubricant*

for life. The reception boy
likes talking to foreigners
because the locals won't
shake his hand. He dreams
of showing his paintings
at the Louvre one day. But
here? *Here is a dustbin.*
I'd just been thinking of
how much I love this place
and would really like to
give it a beautiful gift. I
gave him these expensive
headphones I stole once –
take them, they're yours!
I bought the guru's book
published by Penguin,
and these poems – well,
who edits this shit, like,
is the sloppy lineation
intentional? But here's
one line I loved: *a dry*
stick of logic with an
effusion of flowering.

In the gaze of the mango pip
linga, I'd tied a turmeric root
with a yellow knot to a form
unknown, staining the soles
of my feet with golden mud
as the brown strangers lay
prostrate around me. Fuck,
it really is tempting to just
cosplay enlightenment. Back
in my country, which isn't
my country, everything I
own is in cardboard boxes
in four different places, and
I am here. I am right here –
why must I join your guru's
WhatsApp group?

Buddha's compassionate stance

I am surrounded by fading paintings
depicting fallen empires nameless to me
as the woman downstairs shakes fervently
in the name of the One God. My fellow
tourist is debating notions of authenticity
because these paintings, torn, with holes
are not in a cave – no, they're by modernists
who signed Muslim names yet are nowhere
on the wall plaque. Just Buddha again
tempted by sin, faint outlines of foregone
leaves, a little mould, horns and alarms
at a distance. He had his hair cut like
a saddhu and likes to learn about yoga.
He is going to UP in a week or so for the
gigantic pilgrimage. He says all religions
are welcome, but I know, it's a Hindu thing ...
The damaged painting of painted damage
from its inception, a rendition of that subtle
posture of compassion. Glass frame broken,
'Trapping of geese in the lotus lake' held
together with gaffa tape and a plastic bag.
He squints at the ancient dream, a crack

through the naga king's head. Downstairs
the Holy Relics of the Master hum inside a
glass stupa, arranged along the cardinal
points. A marble Buddha with a broken eye,
arms apparently snapped off by aniconists,
looks out toward the six-foot air purifiers.
I give up believing in the aura of old things.
Another wave of tourists enter, forgetting
to leave behind their shoes. There is little
budget for repairs. A 17th-century Persian
tablet concludes, 'The constellation has
reached its zenith,' and the panel after,
'That the world will not befriend you but
you should be merry.' I show this man
paan, take him to market, masjid, mandir,
teach him the words and talk of the world
but this whole time I talk with myself 'bout
how this fucker tried to buy a keffiyeh
to use as a towel! I'd like to mirror Buddha's
compassionate stance, but I'm smoking
enough cigarettes I don't taste the pollution.

Delhi

In the night, the rooftop brimmed with beery
Europeans who had just arrived, laughing about
food poisoning, asking locals, *What is hash?*
One sat with me. He trained AI to do maths,
quickly declaring his theory that religion is why
nothing works here. *See, in the Netherlands …*
He yapped on about shooting lasers through
an atom, how God didn't exist. Nevertheless,
he was leaving tomorrow for a big gathering
of god men in the putrid river. I said goodnight.

In the morning, the queue snaked out from
the subway, jutting across like a wall blocking
the road; mostly men wearing nylon corporate
slacks and black puffer jackets waited for
security to pat them down, before they could
push their way onto the Yellow line. A few
had their phones out, filming the queue, which
confirmed for me this was, indeed, significant.

As an outsider, I am easily impressed, observing
when even locals grabbed their phones, shooting
photos: in the mountains, out from the bushes of
angel's trumpets, a flock of bison breaking the green
road's edge, one after another stepping out from
the bushes … another! One more! Cars stopped
for a few minutes, we all stood staring silently
at the rippling black muscle, sharp white horn …

Downstairs, men in camouflage with long rifles
ambled just beyond the sweet and chaiwalas.
In the early evening, as workers came home,
the main road would fill with traffic, the horns
connecting together in one long hum of irritation.
Facing the road were cramped little restaurants
selling rice, bread, gravy, meat. Big pots and pans
bubbling outward. Colourful kebab in glass cases.

On the metro, my friend cursed remembering
how she'd forgotten to bring her mask. *All of us*
are at risk of catching bronchitis, the window
coloured with pollution. *I've been eating* so
much tofu lately – it regulates your hormones.
Come home, I'll make you hibiscus tea. We sat
as she flicked through health food reels, asking
if I had ever eaten this Japanese sweet potato.

Then I got sick, the heavy coughing (still!)
hocking up phlegm, spit it out in the gutter
with the excess paan, the ends of tea, plastic
wrappers and dog shit. With only a week left
travelling, I wondered if I'd be stuck in bed.
The novelty had gone – that was desirable.
When the romance wore off, what was left?

Downstairs, a big pot froths with milky tea
separated into a thermos, which pumps out
paper cups of creamy chai for a golden coin.
A man buys a single, lights up by the roadside

puffing and sipping until both cup and butt
are thrown into rubble. He walks into the crowd
of twenty-somethings, toothless uncles and blind
dogs with dreadlocks hanging from their tails.

Indians like to ask me what I've seen while I am here,
which states I have been to, which foods I have tried.
They ask of my religion, if I'm married. Isn't it lonely
travelling by myself? A few days left here, I try
with my collapsing immune system, to see a few
more sights. I visit Qutb Minar, perhaps because
apparently a site in Agra just got bulldozed.

Across from the minaret, the foundations of another
made of raw stones jammed together, was left un-
finished. There was no Persian calligraphy or perfect
tessellations, just stones big enough to wonder how
they were broken, carried – on whose shoulders?
In this society so cast in its famines, someone had
to preserve half-made relics like this, dig them
out from beneath peasants' houses, write reports,
conserve and insure them, get them world-certified.

Tourists come to pose for photos against the pillars. A charming smile, tilted sunglasses. Their hands gesturing in front of the landmark as if it was only bite-size. All of them trying to absorb the dignity of the patrons for a fallen regime. Children run about. Outside, the auto drivers shout prices to take me back to the metro. I pay more than my first offer because I am stubborn and say no too much.

That night I dream of Old Delhi where babies' graves clutter in a butcher's shop, where the slop of cement squeezes out from bricks walls into medieval dargahs of forgotten saints. I dream winding alleys of shadowy encroachment. I dream of getting out, back to dead streets where I'm from. I dream the relief that history is over, that I can breathe. I wake up feeling weak.

traffic saga

To return to a place that I have already written is to return lighter. Undistracted. More involved with the being of the place. I travel a distance to make this uneasy pilgrimage, then remain distant, attempting to be involved. Guarding against my own nature, to forget where I am, disrespect, disenchant, or disavow where I am. It is in this state of a cautious narrative falling into place that I receive the poem. The insight of what is here trembling gently like gut strings between the fingers. This time, there was no need for that. I walked in circles until the Naam leapt out at me. I was here, exiting the langar with a stomach full of saag, rice, beans, bread and pudding. The Golden Temple cracked my heart again. Long dewy tears divided my face into a neat grid. I left a part of me there that murmurs constant prayers while the old thick bearded men stroke phoenix feathers on dear books. The next day, I decided I wouldn't go back, I'd be mundane. All my trip I'd collected books everywhere I went – at least one or two in each town. Bookstores are like cities: imported franchises beside local classics, old hymns, the story behind the grand statue of that king. Indeed, I was amazed how many books were exclusively here – all written or translated into English, the link language (no longer Persian, not yet Hindi). English bookstores towering in disarray, to fossick through for hours each day. This was my peculiar way to practice tourism,

yet it worked. Before even buying anything,
I read bookstores like tea leaves: guessing
why this one lacked a local imprint, stocked so
many self-help books for first-time investors,
built pillars out of Musk and Tata biographies,
had a full splay of Bihari yoga manuals.
I noticed Orwell's 1984, but never *Homage to*
Catalonia, Kafka's *Metamorphosis* but never
The Trial. Candy-coloured covers of Japanese
novels were common. Poetry always got a little
lost in the classics. Religion and philosophy
were interchangeable. Every bookstore seller
had *Autobiography of a Yogi*, Sadhguru, Osho,
Vivekananda and Gandhi. I wish I'd wanted
to buy more copies of the *Ramayana*, as those
were always the most beautiful books. I bought
academic presses on caste and liberation
struggles. I bought many copies of Ambedkar
for everyone to read: books so important that
lakhs of publishers printed their own edition.
His face on the front cover of each copy, such
that now I noticed the statues, his arm reaching
out holding the Indian Constitution, above the
entrance to railway stations, or amidst gods
in the framed picture shops. There he was,
proclaiming a new India in the heritage town
of Amritsar, down the street from the martyrs
of Jallianwala Bagh, accrued in marble flame.
A ladder was propped up on his shoulders –
it was Republic Day, so garlands of marigolds
would settle onto his shoulders. I passed again

at night: flowerless, just police buzzing around suspicious. After briefly watching confused, I carried on home. All this came to mind the next day, stuck in traffic, trying to get to Crossword (a popular franchise where I could buy a few last tomes). My friend sent me a reel of a man with a hammer, going at Babasaheb's face before being dragged away – oh! Arriving at the mall with the bookstore inside, the security guard tells me they'll be closed until 1pm. Then the next guard says 4pm, and the last? Closed all day – and I don't have all day, I have a flight to catch. I walk off, first annoyed then amused by all their contradictory answers, how Google said the store was open? No, India is not for beginners – the perennial mantra of anyone who wants to stay sane while navigating this haywire accretion of half-baked bureaucracies brimming with inefficiency. Shit, I shouldn't say it that way – I'm not stuck living here, I can always leave. But sometimes I get pissed off trying to do something simple, like asking when a store opens. Somehow, that also is too confusing! I paced off down the street around an area that looked nothing like the mall, found a roadside juice shop, ordered a large orange juice. The pulp on top tasted bad, bitter, but the rest of the cup was glory. Content to now book another moto on Rapido, I turned down the next street, pulled out a Gold Flake Lite ... The rev of a bike interrupted. (Indeed, often everything is quite loud, but it would be too hard to write that into every sentence.) Taking his helmet off, he is cleanly shaved but for a large moustache. Stating plainly, 'I am police,' he takes out his wallet to show me an ID card, 'I am police.' Caught holding my cigarette, I look at him calmly. 'Yes, uh ... Do you want me to put this away?' A firm nod, 'Not allowed.' 'Sorry, I'm happy to put it away.' He seems like he'll drop it. I feel innocuous in my white shirt. 'Why are you here?' Yes. 'I wanted to visit the mall.' He recognises now, 'Ah. Today is strike, no mall!' Meekly, I hold up the iPhone screen showing a driver approaching. The interaction winds up, he rejoins the road. My moto arrives to take me 7 kms to Books Punch (Google Reviews images of downlit, sunny-coloured shelves, 4.6 stars shining because 86 happy users left many kind words) and approaching the centre of the tier-2 city – well, this much traffic is unusual! This is like the big city traffic that made me miss my train in Bangalore, traffic that kills people stuck in ambulances while motorbikes crawl past. Is it because it's a public holiday? We swerve to the side of the road, up on the footpath in a snake of bikes, passing buses so cramped they could contain companies. Several men are lounging out on the roof. All the cars, buses and trucks have stopped, the autos are jammed, motos stop-and-start. Wind. He goes down one road

then pulls back – whole road has gone dead
in its tracks, so he swerves into the gutter
beside oncoming traffic. (Where I'm from,
only police cars in chase could do this. It makes
sense here though ...) He is on a call the whole
time. His wife maybe, or family. We drive up
another bridge then we're clear, out of the city,
amidst nicer houses. Amritsar posh. A brick
wall with cast-iron spearheads. I notice it is a
school, the uniforms running past the window.
The bookstore has a colourful children's
section, plenty of stationery. At the very back,
a jumble of popular non-fiction, a few novels –
nothing good. Thus began a sinking guilt that
I made this driver shove through all this traffic,
for what? I leave the store, calling him back,
and after lying to him that I found the book
I was looking for, we fall back into the wind,
lurching traffic beneath the flyovers' shadows,
and he asks if it's okay to drop me here, right
in the mess of it – he points, 'Quicker to walk,
just over there,' and I'm off the bike pushing
past autos with Moose Wala decals, Vishnu's
quiver, colourful convoys with All India Permits
and the odd white BM stuck behind my out-
held palm as I squeeze between the bonnet
and a flatbed truckload of workers, I presume,
going somewhere. (I may have lost the point
of this story in the traffic). There is a leak on
the road back home, creating a large puddle

that can only be crossed at certain points. Someone has pushed a hessian bag into the mud, a makeshift bridge that I used last night. Now it's almost lost to the shit – but it's enough. There is an informal recycling hub just outside the hostel, yesterday sorting glass, now paper: pictures of Modi, Amit Shah, president Murmu with children's scribbled lines in cheap colour pencil. The chaiwala smiles at me, an older lady in a simple patiala, her dupatta balancing on a lifetime of womanhood. 'Ek chai,' I smile back holding out the ₹20 ready, and she insists on dusting my seat before I sit down for one last chai – the final star in the incomplete constellation of roadside teashops growing distant now. With each sip, looking slowly at the ochre dirt roads, same colour as the dogs stretched out on their back in the sun, in a pile of foregone plastics and other litter, as workers pull past in a mini lorry, their eyes wide as mine when I first arrived, looking at me the way I look when visiting a temple. I wave back, finishing my cup, call a car, collect up my cargo: 30 kgs of luggage this time, two months of not knowing how to answer when locals ask why I'm here. Fuck, I don't know why I'm in Australia either, but when I'm here I know why people stare. No wonder I like to travel – I'm still transitioning. He pulls up, white sedan, neat turban, long beard insisting that next time, I could just get a moto. The fucking ingenuity! The traffic is nowhere

to be seen, so I ask, 'Wasn't there big traffic
today?' 'Yes,' he answers, 'Strike today, big
protests.' I'm surprised, shuffling my memories
quickly. 'Whole city strike?' 'Yes, someone hit
a statue of – ah!' 'Ambedkar?!' The narrative
of the poem knocks me in the face. 'Yes, he
is a very good man. He did so much for us, so
everyone angry he was disrespected.' I tell him
I know of him, I read his book, I saw his statue!
All the police – so strange ... The roads clear.
I will be hours early. I could end this poem now.

He smiles at me, happy I know his name, read
his book, love his people. He is interested in why
I am here. We do not stop talking until we get
to the airport. He helps with my luggage. I give
a big tip, and we both are grinning. 'Well ...
thank you,' and I wheel off the baggage trolley
out of the informal, unlicensed halfway zone
of the parking lot, toward the arrivals gate that
looks like anywhere. Chai outside is ₹40, but I
want to get past security – men holding guns
who must see my ticket and passport. Another
gun pointed directly at the entrance, behind
a wooden screen. 'Hey, please scan your bag
through here!' The procedure is all different.
A white plaster replica of a Golden Temple sits
in an acrylic display box, and then another one
bigger than the last, yellowing to gurus' hymns
over the speaker. Behind that is a shop selling
Australian cookies – only, they have no cookies

and a full South Indian menu. It is unstaffed and the chai is ₹120. That's 300% inflation compared with outside. I am about to ascend the mountain of price as I leave this country. I ask when the counter opens – not for another hour. I sit on the floor with my phone plugged in to a pillar, still in India I guess, but really just waiting to leave now. About 30 hours till I'm home ... Wasting time on phone games. I look up and the queue has begun. I approach, and am told to join a different queue – the official queue for baggage scanning, bending broken here and there. A big baggage scanner unlike anything back home, and after it goes through once – 'What is that there? Take that out. We have to rescan it.' It's a portable speaker. Third time lucky, it's cleared. They put little stickers on each of the bags, then I'm back at the first queue, jerking toward the desk. Queues in India are as strange to me as some exotic religious ritual, they seem lost in a history I can't begin to decipher. I would read a book on queueing in the subcontinent. Did the British do this too? Next to the queue, another short line builds up squeezing toward the first whenever someone reaches check-in. Line dividers are abruptly lifted as some are let through, while others stand at the desk, passports unfolded, staff gathering around looking at the screen, unsure. A machine beside the queue spins long sheets of plastic film around a suitcase, two souvenir horses in an unknown folk art style. Another jolt forward, I write another line. I am counting how many more will need to be served before I get up front. Eight. Seven. Six. Over there, a man gets in a screaming match with an attendant and everyone looks. At this point, I think about the noise outside, how it has re-entered the space momentarily, before guards escort him out – 'Next please!' I turn back, pushing the trolley to the counter, get out my passport and e-ticket. Locals carry folders full of printed tickets, visa forms, identification documents and perhaps even multiple passports. I lift the luggage, momentarily anxious that even though I bought more weight, it's still too much. 'Okay Sir!' The printer gurgles in confirmation. 'This is your boarding pass. You can go straight to immigration,' his hand gesturing past the desk. Elated, I leave arrivals, have my boarding pass stamped, and join another queue: baggage scanner, the third. There are very few trays. Security is yelling out, *Batteries! Computers! Anything sharp or flammable!* And yell it again. Men raise arms, patted down, while women step aside in a curtained-off cubicle. The metal detector beeps and the man remembers his belt buckle. Bags are scanned, disassembled, one item removed and scanned again. What is so Indian about this? I don't know, perhaps it's how common it is: every single mall has a metal detector that beeps as security pushes you through; every train station, even metros, scan baggage and pat you down. I had to ask about this. 'Do you think it really stops anything?' He laughed. A sort of performance of safety, maybe less for spotting danger than reassuring the scared. 'You have a lighter in your bag?' airport security asked, insisting that no lighters were allowed. I took it out of the bag, rescanned, and was allowed through, without having it confiscated. Another layer past, finally at immigration, two lines with no signage snaked to the desk. I joined the shortest only to realise it was being served by one desk while the longer was seen by four. Confused, I asked a service staff member who told me, 'Don't worry, uh, you're in the right place!' an awkward smile, a statement so broad, it could stretch over my entire trip. ('Matlab', the Hindi word for meaning, purpose, from Persian, Arabic.) I transcend to the front of the queue. People who entered the other queue are already ahead of me, pushing their thumbs into the scanner, and smiling at the Logitech webcams. He waves me forth from the queue. 'Passport, please,' I hand it over. Last time, I watched a man get told his visa wasn't up to date, and while I received my stamp, he was walked off by staff, back towards the gates. 'Where did you visit?' security asks in plain, sombre fashion, shirt and tie, slacks — authority. I wonder how much I should tell him. 'Chennai,

Bangalore, Kerala, Hyderabad, Nagpur, Delhi, and Amritsar.' When I say it like that, it sounds both too much and not enough. What does he learn from this list? Who am I to him? 'Oh, you have visited so many places.' I can't tell if he's pleased, jealous or suspicious; the dead tone of the final border before I am in true purgatory in airport lounges, layovers, long pockets of cramped air pumped – with a heavy thump, the stamp goes down the first time, again, and he hands back the passport, wishes me a safe flight. One always passes the duty-free shops feeling elated, lighter. In a little bar fridge, they sell single beers to drink mid-flight. You aren't allowed to drink them in the terminal though … A news story I read: Gujarati businessmen leaving their dry state for some Gulf country drink the whole plane dry and vlog drunk – it goes viral, in a country where drinking is still often frowned upon; the shady liquor shops where throngs of men push past each other to get drunk at home, because there aren't any pubs. I think of how it must feel to leave a homeland like this. I begin feeling the full stop of this trip, waiting for staff to re-emerge at the bar. I submit to the airport prices, laying waste to whatever cash is left in my pockets. I order the same extra-strength beer stocked at my local curry shop, Haywards 5000. I like how it sounds, like a model of vacuum. Every time I order it, they look a little concerned, ask if I know what I'm in for. Yes. She pours a plate full of peanuts and pops the tall bottle top. Now I sit in the bar stall, a simulated place just like the Golden Temple replicas, sit in the heaviest beer taste, enjoying the luxury of Australian alcoholism, that semblance of culture, as I begin to consider what coming here means, what I had done with my time. I guess the trip had died, laid out on a table leftover memories ripe to be diced, dissected. I lift the long neck in a soft salute to the businessman in the next stall. I often wonder if men like this have more than me, or less. More privilege, more access, more money. I still can't tell where I am in this world, what I have and what I lack; in 3AC class, sleeping beside five other Nigerians, every one had brand new iPhones. It is so normal to ask, *are you here for work or just travel*? But nah, we didn't talk once ... Beery, I return to the barmaid. 'Chicken 65?' she runs out back to make sure they can make it, then quotes a price more than the menu – even in airports, price is negotiable? I insist on the menu price, pay, and ten minutes later the dish comes out drowning in oil and chilli sauce. Now I watch the time, flagellating myself with thoughts of missing my flight. I scoff my last meal here, walking tippled to the gate where they queue. I've never understood the impulse to rush to board a plane; after all, seats are ticketed, luggage is measured and weighed, lift off and landing is the same for all. I watch the queue for a couple more minutes, then when it really moves, I get in line. The night is collapsing like a vacuum into the Boeing. The air hostess matches my ticket with my passport, and rips the stub. 'Thank you,' she repeats, gesturing to the airbridge. Another queue, this time filled with small children ignorant of what they are about to undertake. Two toddlers chase each other, then are yanked back in place. Shuffling forward, to the next hostess who checks the seat number: all the way to the back. I stop and start as luggage is pushed around, legs are climbed over, passengers getting up and down to make way for one another, all the way to the back. The row is empty. Stowing my bag and throwing my book on my seat, I sit by the window, unlace my shoes and settle. Maybe I'll get the whole row, maybe I'll really fall asleep ... 'Cabin crew arm doors cross check,' the same rhythm that coaxed me as a child begins the ritual of the inner sanctum of liquid capital. Air is pushed in as the cabin pressurises, and two seats space stretch before me – ah, luxury is not available to buy, it's just good luck. I unfold my book, return to the middle of an epic – but a mother and her crying baby walk the aisles then as the safety demonstration begins, and the plane starts taxiing, she sits besides me, dad close behind, both trying to coo the little one into sleep: many pats; soft voices; offering of a breast; 'What about white noise?' Dad loads YouTube, scrambles the search, pressing play, and a Nivea whitening lotion ad lulls the baby to – no. Fuck. The air hostesses, arms out towards emergency exits. He rushes back to his seat, more kids. She starts humming. I've given up on my book. This is better, this is real. She and the baby lock together, and then I feel it, start humming too: hmmmmmmmmmmmmmm (as long as my breath will allow) hmmmmmmm mmmmmmm (the baby is falling asleep while breastfeeding) hmmmmmmmmmmmmmmmm (mother and I nod at each other) hmmmmmm mmmmmmm (it must have been a few minutes like this) hmmmmmmmmmmmmmmmm (truly the baby seems at peace) hmmmmmmmmmm mmmmmm (the vibration in the cavern of my mouth) hmmmmmmmmmmmmmmm (the rattle of the jet begins) hmmmmmmmmmmmmmmmm mmmmmm. Lift off, and the baby's still asleep.

ACKNOWLEDGEMENTS

This book owes so much to so many. To my partner, Tara Denny. To Batool Ali, Holly Callec, Stacey Collee, Jack Doepel, Naveen Navi, Ella Parkes-Talbot, Divya Phillip, Juliet Phraser, Aisha Sajmi K, Andina Setyowati, my co-workers, friends at Arayie, Delhi Queer Heritage Walks, Library Portal and the many others who may see themselves reflected in my poems. To my mum, for so much encouragement and proofreading. To Alex Creecc, Elena Gomez, Kent MacCarter, Autumn Royal and Lucy Van for all their support.

'half-written poem' was first published in *The Suburban Review*, edited by Claire Albrecht. The chapter 'consecration' was first published in *Cordite Poetry Review* as 'Sanskari Girl'.

Thank you to all the venues and organisers who helped find these poems their audiences, including Dinner Party Press, Footscray West Writers Fest, KalliopeX, no more poetry, No Place, Audrey Pfister, the Wheeler Centre's Next Big Thing and the Williamstown Literary Festival.

Lia Dewey Morgan is a poet and emerging librarian based in Naarm. She is a proud trans woman of Anglo and South Asian heritage. She is a 2024 Wheeler Centre Hot Desk Fellow, and a founding member of the independent community initiative Library Portal.